Boomerang Girl

JOHN RENNELL SECOR

Order this book online at www.trafford.com
or email orders@trafford.com

Most Trafford titles are also available at major online book retailers.

© Copyright 2017 John Rennell Secor.

All rights reserved. No part of this publication may be reproduced, stored in a retrieval system, or transmitted, in any form or by any means, electronic, mechanical, photocopying, recording, or otherwise, without the written prior permission of the author.

Print information available on the last page.

ISBN: 978-1-4907-8138-9 (sc)
ISBN: 978-1-4907-8137-2 (e)

Library of Congress Control Number: 2017903618

Because of the dynamic nature of the Internet, any web addresses or links contained in this book may have changed since publication and may no longer be valid. The views expressed in this work are solely those of the author and do not necessarily reflect the views of the publisher, and the publisher hereby disclaims any responsibility for them.

Any people depicted in stock imagery provided by Thinkstock are models, and such images are being used for illustrative purposes only.
Certain stock imagery © Thinkstock.

Trafford rev. 03/29/2017

Trafford PUBLISHING www.trafford.com

North America & international
toll-free: 1 888 232 4444 (USA & Canada)
fax: 812 355 4082

Contents

Boomerang girl 1
Two little boys and a girl 2
What hath God joined together? 3
Mouvances 4
A cameo of Margaret, in memoriam 6
Joan Baez in concert 7
A Love Poem 8
On my birthday 9
I don't… 10
Of a Sunday morning in December 11
Glory, glory, hallelujah 12
Homework at the boys' school, October 1972 13
She flies through the air… 14
Pick-up or take-out at B-dubs 15
For my brother Peter, as he turns sixty 16
This may sting a little 17
Double switch 18
Parce que c'était lui, parce que c'était moi 19
Looking into medieval Paris from la tour St-Jacques ... 21
The high dive 23
Pat's gone 24
French ladies in the harbor 25
House for sale 26
In a big city church hall, Saturday night 27
Float like a butterfly 28
Phantasme parisien 29

Parisian fantasy 30
Les Filles Monoprix 31
Target girls 32
On ne badine pas avec l'amour 33
Marion 34
In memoriam Bruxelles 35
The Airport Bombing in Bruxelles 36
Down in the river to pray 37
The brick 38
Born to be mild 40
Sandy Hook Elementary 41
Handle with care 42
Surprise at the County Jail 43
Midnight waltz 44
Suitcases 46
Mea culpa 47
Abandonate ogni speranza 48
I feel like a Peeping Tom 50
Harry's tale 51
Translating myself 53
Valentine's Day 55
L'aurore dans le RER 56
Dawning in the express train back to Paris 57

Author bio 58
Acknowledgments 59
Notes 60

for my family and friends

Boomerang girl

*I want to live
with a boomerang girl
I could be happy
the rest of my life
with a boomerang girl*

a great toss
a flick of the wrist
she's out of here, way out, out of sight

into her great outback
climbing Ayer's Rock - Uluru
two-stepping with kangaroos

I respect her coral reef
ancient alive headstrong
her mind a jumble of gemstones
blinding me grinding me

she speaks to the night sky
in aboriginal tongues
she is a wonder down under

whirring spinning in orbit
she's out on her own recognizance

you know and I know
she will return

my boomerang girl

Two little boys and a girl

eyes closed tight her light hair is brown
tiny white booties and knitted clothes
tucked into hand-made soft blanket
white flecked with blue and pink

how did this happen?
won't the doctor make her well?
oh no don't close the lid
on my sleeping sister

her small pearl hand
I'll never take to cross the street
it is warm for December
Dad gets up to play the organ

later, ablutions with little brother
off with the church clothes
into bubbly soothing waters
toy boats and sea creatures

splashing sadness into hilarity
unexpected relief
water washing away dirt and sin
but grief – who knew?

Johanna never took a first breath
the warm placental bath
was her earthly cradle
the tolling of her mom's heartbeat

What hath God joined together?

did you know
way back when
that you were hitching wagons with

a man of wind and fire
to your earth and water
a man of thunder, lightning, and hail
to your open-air, free-range ways
a man obsessed with kitchen crumbs
life's organic leavings
to your oneness with Nature
a man of clutter and paper mountains
to your timely, bottom-line accounting
a man of night visions and day-dreams
to your pinpoint reality
a twitchy man, an itchy man
to your tidal ebbs and flows
a man of excess and insult
to your restraint and quiet
a man of air and bluster
to your wellspring of deep feelings

tell me, did you know all that?

I sure as hell didn't!

Mouvances

Mouvances she said
tell them what it means
how it captures and distills
all those swinging saloon door
adventures and journeys

preliminary note: *mouvances* is French
and rhymes with our word, *onset*
or *aunts*, pronounced the British way

so, what is *mouvances*?
is it stepping through a looking glass
or a wardrobe full of old fur coats?

is it the taste of a spongy cookie soaked in hot tea?
is it like the effects of an opium pipe or a lid of LSD?

not necessarily
for *mouvances* is the archæology of self
a meditation, a release from life's burdens
the restless pursuit of meaning
seeing the past with absolute clarity
even when the future makes no promises

this is the modern human condition
divorced, unemployed, orphaned, homeless
spontaneous dream conversations
with dead friends and family
memories, travels, heirlooms, *Rosebud*

mouvances is the mind like a sailboat
coming about to see the fog lifting
from shores left long ago, now in sharp focus

A cameo of Margaret, in memoriam

my mother is

an enchanted isle
a barrel of monkeys
a perfect coffee soufflé
crest-fallen by her tardy husband
a fusty old gentleman (with a twinkle in his eye)

my mother is

the shore, the hearth, the anvil
upon which that fusty gentleman she unwittingly raised
is buffeted, is stoked, is hammered
by life's vicissitudes and dog poop on the sidewalk
ever forged anew, into the molten embers,
tempered by the might of the world,
soothed by cool waters, steam released

my mother is

a series of coincidences
a high-strung guitar fret
a set of blue and white china
a merry Oldsmobile
nostalgic for Dave Keon (the most elegant Leaf)

my mother is
a Yorkshire pudding, with roast beef, *rare*

Joan Baez in concert

Ashland, KY, February 1994

swing low
you first sang in Sarajevo
sweet chariot
dedicated to the victims of armed conflict
coming for to carry me home
in Bosnia and Herzegovina, Aleppo…

swing low
my wife and I were with friends at the concert
sweet chariot
we listened in rapture, transfixed
coming for to carry me home
by you alone, Joan, center stage, before intermission

if you get to heaven before I do
setting a tone of hope and expectation
coming for to carry me home
your hair now grey and shorter
the café con crema voice singing for justice
tell all of God's angels I'm coming after you

after the concert
seated, legs dangling off the stage
patiently you welcomed your fans one by one
and took our babe of all of three months
held him tightly in your arms as your own
proof that the world will go on

oh Joan, we need you now more than ever!
coming for to carry us home

A Love Poem

At fifty-two, my love, the day is spent
The night is tender; it mocks the deep sleep,
Refashions what was lost, unrepentant:
My soul exfoliated, a clean sweep.

What now, what new, what if these lips I kiss
These hands I hold, these eyes in which I drown,
Drown, drinking, drifting, your features I miss
You, my virtual kingdom's queen, I crown.

Through a screen darkly, myself reflected,
Chained to chair, the French-accented email
Le mot juste, quixotic keystrokes you've read,
What Windows can withstand our hearts' travail?

Is this real or grey foolishness tonight
To you, dearest, my cyber-troth to plight?

On my birthday

a conflicted day umpteen years ago
do we know the truth? a smooth implosion
a third of a mile of glass steel concrete
a plume of smoke, suffocating dust haze
such a bee sting on the epidermis
provokes greater TV terrorism
over and over and over again
ten per cent foreign nationals amongst
almost three thousand patriot bankers
secretaries and doomed first responders
each anniversary grows tiny stars
and stripes, gallant streams across campus lawns

...odd coincidences

November eleventh, my father's birth
six years exactly from the armistice
which curtailed the slaughter of WWI

May thirtieth is Memorial Day
or grandma's birthday in 1904
remembering all those fallen brothers
we hoped, with Lincoln, had not died in vain

nine-eleven, my day, dials pathos
an awkward birthday for celebration
will I ever enjoy my cake in peace?

I don't...

I don't carry

the weight of the world
on my shoulders

the prejudices of my ancestors

the debts of my neighbors

water, grudges

left-over fish, barbed remarks

the regret of not leaving
the last cookie in the jar

unnecessary baggage or burdens

pointed rhetoric
a sharp tongue
retorts, reproaches, resentments

firecrackers, hot coals, home-made shanks

unrealistic expectations

do you?

Of a Sunday morning in December

o.k. so puzzle master Will Shortz
can turn Cate Blanchett
into freedom
carte blanche

after a time
the weekend British soccer din
the NPR news buzz
the Advent wreath lighted

the grinding gears
of global warming
the implacable extremists
of global warning

I must shut off all extraneous sounds
to hear the poetry in silences
to guide our feet into the way of peace
as the *Song of Zechariah* puts it (Luke 1:79)

the Christmas baby we had to bury
how hasn't my life been flipped?
this season of waiting and expectation
light a candle for me, my dearest love

Glory, glory, hallelujah

one day paying my utility bill in cash
along came octogenarian Glenn
the jaunty, one-time chair of Music
he told me how he had been drafted
into the marching band as a boy drummer
Memorial Day in Buffalo, NY
with Doughboys, Roughriders, Indian fighters
no Minutemen – it was 1933, - but
surely ancient Civil War veterans

just to imagine the Blue and the Grey
brothers charging into armed conflict
each side *terrified when they entered the cloud*
as it says in Luke 9: 33

smoke at Gettysburg, Chancellorsville, Antietam
prepared to meet their Maker
shrieks of horses, screams of men
the *hardened minds* of officers
like the Israelites in Exodus 34: 34

unseeing, *a veil lies over their minds*
(2 Corinthians 3:12) as we witness
so many thousand martyrs continue to perish

can we afford *not to pay* the price of peace?

Homework at the boys' school, October 1972

a last-minute weekend assignment for English
write a poem for Monday's class
as if we would bring in a sonnet
an ode for the Canadian literature trophy case
what did Kerr expect from 17- and 18-year-olds
stuck on girls, cars, and *Stairway to Heaven?*

then by Tuesday, to my utter amazement
you immortalized my epigram
in chalk on your blackboard: *do not erase!*
protected, privileged, provocative
my short poem remained all week
a model for boys in other classes

later, almost thirty years later
you attended my father's funeral
and, listening to my epic eulogy
wrote down on a piece of paper
that brief adolescent riddle of mine
and gave it to me - how touched I was!

thank you, Mr. Kerr, for doubly honoring me:

>*ecstasy*
>
>   *marmalade*
>*meanders through my bread and butter*
>*body*
>   *despair*

She flies through the air...

here comes my friend, the lady professor
large round glasses framed by grey locks
ready to read her scholarly paper:
Bahktin's Carnevalesque in the Circus
how acrobats, clowns and wild animals
connect the post-industrial world
to primitive feelings of the unknown

evoking excitement, her own childhood
her father taking her to the Big Top
far-off, post-war Czechoslovakia
a seasoned academic on the high wire
suddenly stumbles hearing her own voice

she grasps for her father's hand to safety
but instead finds the tweedy audience
transformed into a six-year-old's tapestry
of hunger and hurt, heaven and hell
creature comforts and Cold War cares

now she must beg professional courtesy
a colleague gracefully finishes up her tale

Pick-up or take-out at B-dubs

a grey, grizzled professor
savoring a simple pint
& chicken artichoke flatbread
off-night at the sports bar
Westminster Dog Show on all screens

*we now bring you a word
from our sponsors*

free-range chicks
pecking, clucking, grazing
scouring the prairie
strutting their stuff
in his face

tempting
but untouched platter
sweetmeats proffered
to his sober puzzlement
are they real? he thinks not!

who put the *wild* in Wings?
where *do* the buffalo roam?
oh, give those busty girls a home!
please no discouraging word!
no cloudy skies all day, nor night

For my brother Peter, as he turns sixty

the hill behind Gow House drew us like druids
to worship trees, leaves, sun, wind, the red swing set

two other kids gliding back and forth on seats
at four and a half, of course I wanted my turn

clambered onto the swinging bars, holding on
until…I fell, twisting, tumbling, torqueing

Mommy, Mommy! at three and a half, you
the future Foreign Service Officer
ran an urgent mission down the hill
around to the front door up the stairs
into our apartment through the living room
to the kitchen, *John's hurt, come see!*

perhaps you were jealous of my hard cast
heavy plaster-of-Paris; like a turtle I crawled

perhaps you enjoyed shuttle diplomacy
perhaps you learned caution, observation
the rewards of delivering the right message
to the right person at the right time

at three and a half, it was all visible:
your character and personality
devotion to family, stubborn loyalty
the man present in the child

This may sting a little

this may sting a little
he said before pulling the trigger
on his canister of liquid nitrogen
when the dermatologist pays heed
to the well-worn face
surveying like a prospector
an old map, freezing extraneous bits

it doesn't sting like the reflection in the mirror
that can trap you in life-long adolescence
self-doubts now blossom and bloom
just to exist after sixty, keeping ahead of death
sharing a quip with the lawyer
about disposal of your mortal remains and heirlooms

there is no sting there
only the preternatural sounds
of symphony orchestras
angelic choirs taking a big breath
before the baton drops at the first downbeat
the first chord you can clearly hear
even in the soft bed awake at night
awaiting you in silence

Double switch

for Stephanie

when he told you
he loved you no less
but desired to become
a woman

you gave him one of your
Birth of Venus Botticelli looks
wistful and wondering
as time stutters

a puff of air playing with your hair
innocent above the bloody foam
that cruelest cut to Father Uranus
sharp shell shock

a look passed between us as if to say
twin misfortunes yours and mine
love had gone awry – Sarah left me for her
leaving me to question who I am

you give them drink
from the river of your delights *
and find yourself alone on the love seat
watching the dreidels spinning

*Psalm 36: 8

*Parce que c'était lui,
parce que c'était moi*

À la mémoire de DWK, 1956-2012

each rare meeting we caught up with our lives
weird luck again eight days before your death...

in the early 80s when Wayne walked us
me and my lady down from the small flat
through west Philly sweating expectantly
dogs and children carefree in the parklet
he sat stiffly against the iron fence
like a Japanese tea ceremony

I've something to tell you (big breath) *I'm gay*
he said with relief humility fear
how would his best friends from college react?
no worries, just a slight exchange of smiles
oh, Wayne, still my close friend and confidante
eagle scout, opera buff, Francophile, wit

we parroted Monty Python sketches
this was before the AIDS quilt, Harvey Milk
Gay Pride parades, same-sex marriages, Kim
Davis; weren't the 70s confusing:
long hair, flannel shirts and faded genders
moved back and forth as the lines were erased

does a label change who you really are?
I wondered, I worried, I didn't want
to know who was doing what with whom when
whose business *is* sexual preference?
a great friend who can share life's twists and turns
grey professors over pizza and beer

Looking into medieval Paris from la tour St-Jacques

three hundred stone steps in a spiral
my heart climbs up my constricting throat

out into the open damp breezes
twenty-five feet by twenty-five feet

four feet of crenelated parapet
give me a moment with my vertigo

a bewildering view of medieval Paris
Notre Dame, the Seine, arched bridges, narrow streets

below was once St-Jacques-de-la-Boucherie
home parish of Nicolas Flamel (1330-1418)

to whose stone dwelling six blocks north
(the oldest house in Paris) I later convey students

a nice man mopping bistro floors
may we step in for a photo – mais oui bien sûr

she said: *Dr. Secor I didn't know the necromancer
in* Harry Potter and the Philosopher's Stone
actually lived in this house six hundred years ago

and I replied: *Elizabeth I didn't know
Nicolas Flamel the scribe and manuscript-seller
was a character in a famous book by J.K.Rowling*

we turned the same corner and what did we see?
for me the fantasy of palpable history
for her a selfie with a celebrity

The high dive

going on twelve I've got to impress
my friend, *Charles Atlas*, who is just thirteen

one, two, three, four, sprrring!
off the ten-meter board
up into open, humid
chlorinated oh so un-
Toronto-like air in
February above the
blue pool – will I hit the
water? falling in space
ten meters per second squared
shshshoooom! acceleration! splash!

six years later climbing up, up, up to
ten meters freezes me like a popsicle
all those kids waiting below
humiliated I
turn and melt
down in shame

Pat's gone

for Carlton, Katie & Judy

according to Jerry, the lights were on
but no one was home the last few days

Viêt-nam vet, postal carrier
prolific songster, superdad
he fought hard:

pancreatic cancer, two weeks' notice
stretched out to seven
through a winter wild and woolly
not seen in twenty years

his lean, homespun looks put folks at ease
how's mister John today? he would say
I can hear him still, his bluesy, harmonica
mandolin voice, warm grits and crawfish

his thoughts clear, his words true
his heart freely given -
you could tell the man cared -
and as for me, I do not give up
honest friends without a struggle

French ladies in the harbor

it's 1939: New York World's Fair
which showcases the *World of Tomorrow*
Hitler's *Blitzkrieg* into Poland at hand

Marguerite and younger colleague Suzie
teach English in Paris; visit New York
to see lifelong friend and French teacher, Kit

late summer the former set sail for home
below the deserted ship on the pier
my great-aunt Kit DuBois waves a black glove

why won't they stay? – we know what is coming
will the Maginot Line keep out the Krauts?
my brother died in the Great War – who next?

will they live through the suffering, despair?
no heat no meat no subway no coffee
Occupation and Résistance, Vichy

Bartholdi's green lady salutes, torch high
two schoolteachers answering the call home
ration coupons slipped to Jewish children

Bon voyage and farewell; goodbye, *adieu!*
wartime privations do in Marguerite
while Kit succumbs in 1946

bravery may be measured in bullets
real courage cannot be calculated

House for sale

the key turns in the lock
heavy door with three lancet windows
opens into a cool, quiet cavernous space
empty bookcases and narrow plank hardwood floors
shadows where their paintings opened pastel walls
into landscapes – my sons' new realities

an idle chair here and there
where the clan gathered
memories of kneading dough
two dozen baguettes baking
home brew and stone soup
a dog and two cats at rest up the hill

like a vacated hermit crab shell
it echoes inside – life has moved on
the sea the wind the sand cosset it
leaving salt streaks of sweat and tears
when I hold it to my ear I hear crystalline grains
crashing through the hourglass of time

In a big city church hall, Saturday night

bell bottoms
a strobe light
perfumed long hair
two hearts beat to
a whiter shade of pale

at age fifteen or fourteen
what do you learn
from a four-minute
languid slow dance
with an absolute stranger?

Float like a butterfly

when Andrew and Austin
young heavyweight-class beards
stepped into the ring at Pasquale's
banjo and guitar, weaving and bobbing
fingers dancing across the acoustic canvas
channeling Simon and Garfunkle:
in the clearing stands a boxer...
it was a combination punch
little did they realize
how their pure voices *stung like a bee*
and how they *brought some comfort here*
the night before they buried *The Greatest*

Phantasme parisien

tes bas noirs
m'abattent
tes collants
m'accolent
leur alcool
je mijote
je sirote
dans mon bol
tu seras
mon école
frivole
mon cœur
s'envole
mes pas
ne tiennent plus
le sol
Nicole

Parisian fantasy

Nichole
bless her soul
bless her leggings
black as coal
poured like alcohol
filling my bowl
stirring
sipping
knocking me cold
she's taking me to school
that's her role
in pidgin or creole
my heart she stole
swifter than Diana Krall
out of control
I'm paying the toll
have mercy on my soul

Les Filles Monoprix

hey, man !
si on cherche
des filles
Monoprix
qui fréquentent
la laverie
qu'est-ce que ça simplifie
c'est facile la vie
on peut faire des économies
finis les ennuis
n'est-ce pas, chérie ?

sapristi !
je suis cuit !
et à quel prix…
voici ma carte de crédit
ça suffit, je t'en prie !

Target girls

dude !
let's check out
the chicks
at Target
Friday night
laundromat regulars
like, how cool is that
it's a no-brainer
stash some cash
no problemo!
believe me, sweetie

holy crap!
I'm screwed
it's all for you
here's my *Visa*, baby
no more, pleeeeze !

On ne badine pas avec l'amour

pour Marion

si j'osais prendre un menu gastronomique
ou commander un dessert gourmand
comme ma tante anglaise, que cela ne déplaise

peu importent mes angoisses, ma douleur
de ce que tu t'inquiètes pour moi –
la bouillabaisse de mes émotions

une mer calme et rouge qui cache
des morceaux succulents, des coquillages
des surprises aiguës, des arêtes

n'empêche, lorsque tu choisis à la carte
selon ta fougue, tes désirs du moment;
le plat du jour – ça ne te dit plus?

Marion

if I dared order the most expensive full-course dinner
or even a sampler of desserts, just for me
that what my aunt in England would do, no offense

do you understand why I am so heartsick
when you say you're worrying about me -
the bouillabaisse of my emotions

the calm, red sea beneath which hide
the tastiest pieces of fish and shells
some sharp surprises, too, bones

never mind, when you pick and choose off the menu
according to how you feel, your latest crush;
the daily special – don't you want me anymore?

In memoriam Bruxelles

pour TSP, le 22 mars 2016

elle a entendu sonner
elle a décroché à l'aube
elle a reçu le message
une trentaine de morts
victimes au cœur
de son pays d'origine

elle a exprimé à la radio
ses sentiments et ses craintes
sa mère qui rentre par avion
demain au hasard, par chance
qui aurait pu se trouver
en plein danger, qui sait ?

les suicidaires c'est imprévisible
que voulez-vous, il faut faire fi !
chercher sa chope et ses frites
ainsi ne vaincront-ils pas
et au lieu de se reprocher
se rapprocher se rapprocher

The Airport Bombing in Bruxelles

she heard the phone ringing
she picked up at dawn
she got the message
thirty people dead
victims in the heart
of her homeland

she expressed on the radio
her feelings and her fears
her mother going home by airplane
tomorrow, as it happens, by chance
she could have found herself
in grave danger, who knows ?

suicide bombers are unpredictable
but you must go on living life as usual !
have a Belgian brew and french fries
they will not defeat us in our defiance
and instead of finding fault because of difference
come together, all cultures, come together

Down in the river to pray

lock-up after church Sunday, safe from rain showers
horseless carriage pew, side by side by the blustery bluff
the young Samuel Clemens navigated this fearsome stream
(as did my Civil War ancestor, Thornton Rennell)
below us engorged with rain, bursting at the seams
like the prom girls in their tight gowns
a torrential downpour filling dry beds
downhill to creeks into the river

you lift up to the heavens this three-flowered Easter lily
in memory of your parents and of your brother
his casket covered by a high tide of white flowers
he loved to work with white in gardens and landscaping
but alcohol poisoned him at twenty-three, so young

now the waters inundate your heart, sitting here
high and dry behind the historical society in Hickman
where one can ferry to the far side
needling through the riverboats' trail
churning paddle wheel slowly spinning tales
another young man at risk, you lift up your son
on the altar of the criminal justice system

freedom lies beyond the waters
not within the confines of four square, pale blue walls
a sentence imposed, a stretch to be served
the river flows unchained, life goes on

The brick

my heart reads like a school primer to her
she knows how the weekly doses of traditional music
leave a joyful imprint on my ears
dancing grooves on the wax cylinder
I will shortly drag across the state

local author Chris Offutt from Haldeman, KY
inspires a search for fossils from the landscape
wheat-colored, gritty-textured fired bricks
stamped from a factory now only a memory
a physical reminder of hills and hollers

Thursday evening's young string balladeers
cast their spell as I watch and look
now out through the plate glass windows
back and forth Troy's truck at work with its winch
hauling away cars parked in campus tow-zones

it recalls my recent calamity in the creek bed
when Troy responded to his brother's call
my long-ago student who remembered me
and kindly rescued me out where cell phones die
seeking elusive Haldeman bricks

the old red Beetle stopped and parked
waiting, sputtering, forgetful, demented
a willful decision to let go - assisted suicide
to my utter disbelief and helpless regret
it knows it will be left behind here

I witness the gentle gliding forward
slow-motion trajectory across a country lane
accelerating to five miles per hour
like a great male walrus plunging into the sea
tree branches break the fall, skidding into the stream

later I found a souvenir brick broken in two
in amongst cinder block ruins of a house fire

Born to be mild

typical teenaged boy
peach fuzz, sixteen, gangly
looking for adventure
a Friday evening dance
at urban school for girls
dimly-lit basement room

Steppenwolf spinning fast
she agrees to dance
I screw up my courage
do you go here? I chirp
conversation starter
just like Easy Rider

not bad looking she has
long glossy dark hair
glasses maybe, smart
and not unfriendly
shouts over the music
I teach here – true story

Sandy Hook Elementary

off route 84 in Connecticut
before Danbury and the NY line
the Blue Colony Diner at Newtown
you can get spanakopita, moussaka
cannoli, grilled cheese – 24/7

a classic boxy diner, gleaming chrome
giant, foil-wrapped iced carrot cake
vinyl booths, tables and chairs for 150
a squad of starched female servers
the watchful owner who thanks each customer

celebrity photos on the walls, and
a local newspaper story about
how they fed all the families
who flew in from afar for the 26
Sandy Hook Elementary funerals

shell-shocked into stunned silence
good food, encouragement and a little time
acted as a salve, loosened tongues
gently pushed aside the barriers of grief
and strange horrifying scrutiny of the world

talk and stories, some laughter even,
as if by magic enter this safe space
like a fog, lifting voices and
hiding the truth no one can
accept or handle just yet

Handle with care

she isn't shy
grabs me with both hands
limns my spine
bends me to her will
eyes and skims
scans and scours me
every line and wrinkle
under scrutiny
looks me up and down
inside and out
emits a sigh
a rare smile
her ardor for me
in creases
please hold me
don't put me back
on the shelf
between poets
R and T!

Surprise at the County Jail

Darryl at thirty-four years old
steps gingerly into the room
a wide grin creases his face
black hair in snake-like rivulets
sides shaved sculpted scrubbed
piercings and tattoos of course

a sleeveless leather jacket
one of the *untouchables*
class D felons in the Workhouse
non-violent drug offenders
receiving family Sunday
afternoon contact visits

small sack brought by sister-in-law
inspected approved with a wink
by Correctional Officer Jim
Darryl kneels before his kids' mother
will you marry me, Meaghan, he asks
she leaps into his arms, *sure will!*

her elation draws tears from her kin
in utter amazement we all turn
as Darryl puts the ring on her finger
we witness a beautiful moment
joy and devotion amid cinder blocks
just like lovers at Tintern Abbey

Midnight waltz

listen up Nadell Fishman!
your *Drive* poems woke me at 3 a.m.
a luminous insight into my Toronto youth

Pushcart prize-worthy no doubt except
two sunlit days racking my brains
to find the lost memory:

was it Susan my BFF at age seven
my mother's forgotten Jewish roots
my film education at the Silent Cinema?

or running up Bay Street at 4:30 a.m.
in Lincoln's post-apocalyptic one-reeler
dear deaf Dolli at the wheel of the Nova?

the Anglican choir school training
in psalm-pointing and breath control
the subway girls who commuted my sentences?

was it Dr. Davis adjusting my new retainer
his eyes glued to the tiny black and white TV
the moment Paul Henderson scored his epic goal?

was it Manuel de Falla's *Miller's Dance*
I nailed on the piano at the Royal Conservatory
as the penultimate performer from our studio?

was it the hours I spent at the Eglinton rink
learning to lift the puck off the ice
to make the thwack sound of adulthood?

please please Nadell
next time you visit
remind me to take notes!

Suitcases

En voilà encore un que les Boches n'auront pas, ca. 1943

Marianne, statuesque, nineteen
steps down off the train from the south
into Paris, *gare Montparnasse*
a law student's purposeful stride

two suitcases are a burden
papa Émile the judge grabs one
as they leave track six towards the street
to fade into the evening fog

...Ingrid Bergman, *Victor Laszlo*...
suddenly a raised black glove, *Halt!*
a stern Gestapo voice stops him
opens his suitcase then and there

passersby wonder: *is he doomed?*
surprise! frilly undergarments
nightgowns and stockings tumble out
Dumkopf! the duped Germans grumble

while Marianne's bag steals away
meat, cheese, eggs from the country farm
elude evil eyes and escape
a slight upward curl in her lip

there's another good one the Krauts won't get!

Mea culpa

I apologize
Denise Levertov
for walking out
in the middle
of your reading
in nineteen seventy-six

it wasn't you
I had a girl problem
nascent love
had me twisted in knots
my obsession
with total presence
absolute absence

the other becomes oneself
there wasn't room for you
at my inn Ms Levertov
funny that's in the past
poetry is now my obsession

girls must wait

Abandonate ogni speranza
O voi ch'entrate!

---

after twenty-seven years in my home
hitch up the Conestoga wagon

like Æneas at night leaving burning Troy
stealth, confusion, bittersweet escape
jettison the past, no suitcase with menorah:
prayer shawls, yarmulke, phylacteries

wait! Anchises tucked up over the shoulders
fireman's carry, a bag of old bones, dad
a trove of loose memories and rattled nerves

Alzheimer's patient, a ruse to rescue and release
it's too soon! you said you would come for me next week

a white lie: *come on, we're just going to church*
your mom doesn't get it, sits stubbornly still
yet yields to the TSA lady's firm hand and voice:
honey, this overcoat, just pass through the gate
and I will put it right back on you again!

a metal detector to board the aircraft
to live out her days near her dear daughter
Mom smiles but does she know me?

Anchises annoyed, yanked off his recliner
what the hell's going on!
this isn't what I do after supper!
hey! Put me down!

no concept of urgency, leaving for good
strong, young hands clutch the household gods
security, faith, hope, continuity

dark penance in the flames

I feel like a Peeping Tom

the chink in a pyramid
hot sticky Egypt all around
gnats buzzing in my ears

carefully eyeing the cool universe within
the boudoir, the antechamber
golden Cleopatra or Judith in her bath

where is she
fair, auburn or raven?
now opens the closet door

I remember myself small
getting both parents up
with the help of a smaller boy

as if sucked out of a vacuum tube
the couch of connubial bliss
Saturday's sloth and moist sheets

adult knees at eye level
learning to identify
which parent by skin and hair

Harry's tale

*In memoriam, Lt. George W. Patterson, Jr., Lt. Robert W. Sibinski,
Staff Sgt. Harold V. Stafford (USAAF)*

no more bombs fell - at least on the Third Reich
May twentieth, nineteen forty-five
Harry AWOL to Paris in civvies and *béret basque*
French fluency his cloak of invisibility
the key to the Latin Quarter apartment his talisman
five flights up and an oblique view of Notre-Dame

Suzie's teaching colleague Marguerite
who let her a room and for forty years
exchanged visits with Harry's aunt Kit
having succumbed to deprivations
a year or two earlier under the Occupation
now the reign of unfettered exuberance
Parisian girls brazenly grateful
to G.I.'s behind hedges they say
in the *Jardin des Tuileries* - make love now not war

a solitary B-26 bomber *dixit Suzie*
taking off from near Liège, Belgium
its crew of three, short the Morse code man
a training flight after thirty-eight missions
catastrophe: lightning takes down plane and crew
separately, unwittingly, my father returns to camp
*what the hell! where did you come from!
goddam! there were no survivors from the crash!*

Harry obligated to identify his mates
write letters of condolence to families and fiancées
his punishment from the captain
takes a psychological toll
ce n'était plus le même garçon
war does no one any favors, said Suzie
only late in life do his photos appear
the narrative of his narrow escape

mother why me? Harry asks Carol
she relates to me her first grandson
just get down on your knees to thank God
that you came back all in one piece

still later, sometime after Harry's death in two thousand
my French students listen to my story unfolding
how young they are, how remote this must seem!

I am because of what he did, and didn't do

Translating myself

obviously my friend the photographer
had the closing reception at the Arts Center
Rowan County's Courthouse built in 1899
her show a patchwork of farms and critters
steep sterile hills planted with tobacco and cows

a non-native herself, cross-pollinated
adapted to Hairpin-Turn County
grafted onto the old place, a transplant
locals request her to record funerals
so careful and considered is her eye

her best friend out of Harlan in attendance
Poet Laureate of Kentucky obviously
calls me out – knows my name – obviously
how did you translate your French poems into English
"the translator is a traitor" Dante's *traduttore traditore*

abandon the literal way let your emotions play
just as my night visions drive me regularly west
overshooting my heart's geographic destination
how did I end up in Iowa? oops! two states too far
rather than my new Jackson Purchase home

translatio the transfer of saints' relics
to a farther shore a new beginning
so too the bilingual poet dreams afresh
destination unknown - *I'm at where I going*
as my youngest son puts it so well,

leading one's thoughts, feelings, soul searchings
from one desert island across seas of doubt and adversity
to a new place under a different sun, a new idiom

Valentine's Day

Mocking Jay
sits back
in her rocker
all alone
comforted
by the deep silence
the frenzy oozing
out of each pore
her hair dark henna
a West Virginia cascade

her history a series
of push pins
over bumpy roads
a map of cross-overs
butterfly interchanges
slippery on-off ramps
eyes closed
in sleek armor
she sees her path
clear to freedom

for DR

L'aurore dans le RER

c'était un soir caniculaire
par un petit air de mystère
je n'étais pas sûr de te plaire
début juin dans le RER

doucement en raccompagnant
ma tante de quatre-vingt-deux ans
visiter ses petits-enfants
des jumeaux de trois mois seulement

sur mon épaule tu poses ta tête
sans mot dire, gentillesse complète
tes paysages riches et honnêtes
la douceur de ton cœur est nette

Dawning in the express train back to Paris

it was hot and tired that evening
we hadn't known each other long
did you like me? – I wasn't sure
early June and the train was lethargic

slowly, slowly, without air conditioning we rode
with my eighty-two-year-old French aunt
after a day in the country visiting
her infant, twin grandsons

as you lean over, your head on my shoulder
no words exchanged, the gesture is clear:
how rich and noble your inner landscapes
your heart kind, sweet and mine

~ ~ finis ~ ~

John Rennell Secor, a native of Poughkeepsie, NY, was raised in Toronto, Canada, and studied at Hobart College in Geneva, NY, The University of North Carolina at Chapel Hill, and in Strasbourg, France. His teaching career took him to Washington state, Pennsylvania, Kentucky, and frequently to Paris in summers. He has travelled extensively in France, and also into other cultures and languages. Always interested in words and language, Secor began as a poet with early pieces in English. Later, professional and personal pursuits led to a long series of poems in French, resulting in a bilingual collection, "Dessert du soir / Evening Sweets," published by Pippa Press in Paris in 2013. More recently, Secor has devoted himself to writing poetry in English about memory and transitions. Secor now lives in west Kentucky, where he continues his enthusiasm for long walks, soccer and singing.

This series of new poems explores love and loss, friendship and transitions, looking backwards through time and outwards to new horizons, always trying to say more by saying less.

Acknowledgments

The author gratefully recognizes the following journals where certain poems have previously appeared: *Inscape*, "Mea culpa," *Pegasus*, "Of a Sunday morning in December."

Thanks also to the many coffee shops, bakeries, cafés, bookstores and pubs – you know who you are, - where I've worked at my craft, one chocolate scone, one latte, one pint at a time, often finding inspiration, or rather, achieving clarity and concision within chaos.

Thanks also to the following who have read and/or listened to and/or critiqued my poems in embryonic or fully evolved forms: the Green River Writers (under the tutelage of Mary O'Dell), the Kentucky State Poetry Society, George Eklund, Gary La Fleur, Mary Jo Netherton, Jeff Peters, John Kerr, Brigitte Peltier, my sons Michael and James, Ben Hawkins, Michael and James, Ben Hawkins, Lauren Decker, Thérèse Saint-Paul, Valérie Hensley, and Janice, above all. Also deserving of thanks for their support during the process of maturing as a writer are Martin & Patsy Tracy and my friends at St. John's and St. Alban's. My late parents, Margaret and Harry, were my foundation, and they continue to inspire me.

Special thanks go to my friends in France, who have welcomed me and my family with open arms over the years, and whom I consider family to me: the late Chantal Rivaud (1924-2017), Jean-Michel and Christèle Rivaud, the late Suzanne Mespoulet (1907-2002), Philippe and Nathalie Charnotet, Albert and Lily Veit.

Notes

"Boomerang Girl." The bass intro to "Cinnamon Girl" inexplicably rolled around my head as I first worked on this poem. Thanks, Neil Young!

"A Cameo of Margaret." (1928-2009) N.B. Dave Keon, #14, an exquisite skater, high scorer and gentlemanly hockey player for the Toronto Maple Leafs of the Glorious 1960s.

"Homework at the boys' school." For those readers not of my vintage, I feel obliged to identify this anthem of my adolescence: *Stairway to Heaven*, by Led Zeppelin, which I remember one lunch time playing gloriously from both ends of my freshman dorm floor.

"For my brother, Peter." Gow House (rhymes with "how now") is a large, 19th century, three-story home which housed three families, one per floor. We inhabited the 2nd floor, near Vassar College, Poughkeepsie, NY, 1959-62. Gow House is also the setting for "I feel like a Peeping Tom."

"Parce que c'était luy, parce que c'était moi." The quotation which titles this poem is from Michel de Montaigne, *Essais* I, xxviii, 3rd ed., 1595. The allusion is to Étienne de la Boëtie, a poet, contemporary, classmate and great friend of Montaigne from Sarlat, in SW France. De la Boëtie died young, at 30 years of age.

"French ladies in the harbor." *The Statue of Liberty*, by Frédéric Auguste Bartholdi (1834-1904), was a gift from France to honor America's Centennial in 1876. France remains the only major European country with whom the USA has never been at war.

"In a big city church hall." *A Whiter Shade of Pale*, by Procul Harum.

"Float like a butterfly," and *sting like a bee*, perhaps the most famous of many [often rhyming] phrases by Muhammed Ali (1942-2016), who also said, with justification, *I am the greatest*.

"Phantasme parisien," "Les Filles Monoprix," "On ne badine pas avec l'amour," "In memoriam Bruxelles," and "L'Aurore dans le RER," were all written by the author, first in French, with English versions later on, to aid in comprehension by those whose French is a bit rusty. The English is not an exact or literal translation of the French, for the author has attempted to capture the spirit, the essence of what originally moved him to write in French, his language of much inspiration and poetic creation.

"On ne badine pas avec l'amour," (You shouldn't trifle with love) references the 1834 play by Alfred de Musset of the same name.

"Les Filles Monoprix/Target girls." The author has taught numerous times in a summer Study Abroad program in Paris for American students (KIIS). One day in Intermediate French class, two male students complained that sophisticated young ladies were inaccessible, out of reach. Without missing a beat, a third male student suggested that they look at the discount store *Monoprix* for girls with less expensive tastes.

"Born to be mild." A play on Steppenwolf's tune, *Born to be wild*, theme song for the 1969 film, *Easy Rider*.

"Midnight waltz." I'm afraid I will need to identify for non-hockey fans that the magnificent left winger Paul Henderson scored three key late goals to secure victory for Canada in the epic and epochal showdown series with the Soviet Union, in September 1972.

"Suitcases." *En voilà encore un que les Boches n'auront pas, ca. 1943*. This expression I have heard used by at least three different French citizens, all born between 1920-50, and uttered specifically and spontaneously after quickly eating a scrumptious pastry! The more polite variant is "Les Allemands," *The Germans*, while I have also heard a historical reference to the Alsatian *ad hominem*, "Le Hitler," *Hitler*, with its diminutive article, *le*.

The filmic, clipped tone of the poem (elaborated from an anecdote by Chantal) not withstanding, the grim realities and deadly repercussions of being caught with contraband by the German authorities in Occupied France (read, *Occupied Europe*) cannot be overstated.

"*Abandonate ogni speranza*" (*Abandon all hope, ye who enter here*). A familiar quotation from Dante Alighieri, *Inferno*, canto iii, which is an inscription found over the entrance to Hell.

Æneas was the mythological refugee from Troy who founded Rome; Anchises his father.

"Harry's tale." (1924-2000) This story, which is true, was first told me by a French family friend, Suzie, who appears also in the poem, "French ladies in the harbor." Suzie spoke beautiful, fluent English, as well as Spanish. She was a great traveler, and enjoyed visiting the US and Canada during her summer breaks from teaching.